MW01289079

The Perfect Assist:

Placing People in the Right Position to Score in Life

Les Pee Wee Harrison

United   States   Portland   Atlanta   United   Kingdom   Australia

THE PERFECT ASSIST
Copyright © 2014 by Les Harrison.

Published by Up High Publishing House, an imprint of Up High Entertainment Group, a division of HJ Enterprises, Atlanta.

All rights reserved. Printed in the United States of America. No part of this book may be reproduced or transmitted in any form or by any means, electronic or mechanical, including scanning, photocopying, recording, or by any information storage and retrieval system, without the prior permission of the publisher.

Creed, Linda. "The Greatest Love of All." *The Greatest Love of All*. Gold Horizon Music Corp and Golden Torch Music Corp. 1977. 2-5. Print.

Cover design by Gino Design King

Layout by Up High Publishing House

ISBN: 9781499584257

Printed in the United States of America

FORWARD

Many people go through life unaware of how we are connected. There exists, however, some exceptionally rare individuals who assist in creating the very fabric of society. Their purpose is to expand human relationships by consistently weaving the threads that bind us. These are the leaders who serve as guides, encouraging us to expand beyond what we thought possible.

Coach Harrison is one of these gifted connectors, who is able to transcend our differences. He combines his awareness, understanding and vision for human potential to inspire and motivate individuals and groups towards fulfilling their destinies.

It is through team work and collaboration that we will reinvigorate our human organizations to advance forward in the twenty-first century. The growth of the individual will be paramount in this developmental process which needs to include personnel at all levels.

By sharing his hope, courage, and experiences in *The Perfect Assist* and his energetic speaking engagements, Les Harrison motivates people to action for goal achievement. He inspires and challenges them to strive for greater purpose.

It is the multitudes of seemingly small connections that create the most beautifully efficient designs. A great weaver knows that small things can make a huge difference; the touch of a hand, a smile, a kind word of encouragement, or a properly timed rebuke. And when the tapestry is turned, what once was a cloth of random threads has become a mosaic of excellence far greater than we ever imagined. "Dream an unrealistic dream and ask yourself, why not?"

Susan McNiel

Sr. Vice President - Wealth Management
UBS Financial Services Inc.

ACKNOWLEDGEMENTS

I'd like to acknowledge so many people who have inspired this book: Leah M. Harrison, and my team Sharmina, Kierra, Kara, Leslie, Marcellus aka Bopeep, Cheyenne, Payton, Nyema, Nyeshia and Michelle aka Halle.

Without my first coaches (my parents) LG and Shirley Harrison, I would not have received the set up for the perfect pass in life. Within that vein, I must include my first team and siblings Richard, Maurice, Cathy, Lisa, Valerie, Dale, Diana, Gayla, Vicente, and Carla (Boss Lady) as well as my brother-in-laws, sister in laws, nieces, nephews, aunts, uncles, cousins and friends.

I want to especially thank my previous coaches who perfectly assisted me in ways both on the court and in life: Jim Martin, Dan Johnson, Phil Jackson, Mark Vernon, Steve Grant, James Pierce, Jim Shaw, Barry Adams, Chuck Robertson, Nick Robertson, Meadowlark Lemon; Susan McNiel and Roddie Miller.

I cannot leave out the perfect training grounds where hard knocks lessons were learned and connections were made that enhanced my learning experiences: Howard Kennedy Grade School, Central Grade School, Sacred Heart, Creighton Prep, Central High School, Langston University (Oklahoma), Iowa Western Community College (Clarinda) and George Fox College.

The actual teams that passed the ball thereby allowing me to utilize my talents: Sacred Heart, Creighton Prep, Central High School (1980-82), Iowa Western (1982-84), George Fox College (1984-86), Shooting Stars (1986-88), Harlem Knights and Meadowlark Lemon's Harlem All Stars.

I thank the great teachers who encouraged me in so many ways: Bobbie Kerrigan Rawley (Sacred Heart), Bill Laird and Paul Bangura (Creighton Prep), and William Reed (Central High), Hector Munn (GFU), Father Dan Kenny (Creighton Prep).

Finally, my friends who unselfishly passed the ball: Big Nasty Milton McBride, Rogers English, Cornelius Williams, Alex Murphy, Darrick Armstrong, Kenny Matthews, Ricky Allen and Ginger Rogers.

PREFACE

The red, white and blue ball whipped down the court like a hot potato with no one holding on to it for more than a split second. Watching that ball move and get into someone's hands to make a basket, really got my attention. I marveled at how these guys enjoyed passing the ball behind their backs and between their legs all the while setting up their teammates for the perfect shot. It was then that the porch light came on! I found my calling! I wanted to be the greatest passer ever to play the game of basketball.

Now when it comes to passing you can't mimic others. You have to read the defense by knowing your opponents strengths and weaknesses. You have to anticipate roadblocks and know where to get the ball in the right place for success. As a point guard, my team mates needed to trust that I would get the ball to them at the right time, and in the right place. On the same token, I needed them to be in that perfect spot, and make the basket, in order for me to get the assist credit.

From the 5th grade on, I knew I had a special gift when it came to passing the basketball. Guys used to pick me to be on their team because they knew I would make great passes. I really loved this attention and worked at mastering the art of passing. I remember when Magic Johnson jumped on the scene and everyone was talking about him being a great passer. I knew I wanted to be the best. What I didn't know was that before I could even be the best, I had to perfect other areas in my life. I was fortunate to have people who saw something in me that they desired to be a part of improving.

The inspiration for this book came when I realized the number of those special people who have given me perfect assists throughout my life. They paved the way for my success in various ways. If it had not been for them, I may not be the person I am today. I encourage every reader to open your mind to those around you who are in need of the perfect assist. It doesn't have to be behind the back or between the legs passes. It could mean you showing up in that perfect spot for them to have success. There is someone out there who needs your direction, your extra attention and your pat on the back to make it through his day. To those in need of a perfect assist, be inspired to set yourself free from the narrow-minded peer pressure which exists in the multitudes, and open your eyes to see the unseen, hear the unheard, and to apply every possibility to your life. After reading my story, I want you to feel hopeful.

I want you to put your mind at peace knowing that greatness lies ahead.

FAMILY

We were a strange little band of characters trudging through life sharing diseases and toothpaste, coveting one another's desserts, hiding shampoo, borrowing money, locking each other out of our rooms, inflicting pain and kissing to heal it in the same instant, loving, laughing, defending, and trying to figure out the common thread that bound us all together.
~Erma Bombeck

I once heard of a man who said he didn't realize that his family was poor because everyone he knew lived the same way he did. Many of the children in his neighborhood lived in single parent homes. No one owned a car. All of the children wore hand me downs, and most every family received some kind of state aid. All he knew was that despite what society claimed he was missing out on, he knew he had the love of his family. Now this man may have come from a situation that you cannot relate to, but you may know someone who has all of the outward appearances of success, yet lack the foundation of all humanity, and that is love. A person may never realize that they are missing out on one of life's greatest gifts until someone shows them what love feels and looks like.

I was born the second child in a large family of thirteen. My parents worked together to instill values and pride in each of us as we navigated through the ups and downs of life's journey. We didn't have all of the latest gadgets, toys or flashy clothing. We didn't live in a house on a hill, or drive in a late model vehicle. What we did have was a sense of security that regardless of our status in life, we knew our parents believed in us, and would do all that they could to help us be successful. I am thankful for the many life lessons that I've learned from my parents who have showed me the true meaning of love.

LG Harrison (My Dad)
"Follow instructions"

My parents have been married for 51 years. Although we did not have a lot, material wise, my ten brothers, sisters and I were fortunate to have a stable home environment with a homemaking mother, and a strong father who led the family.

My father was my role model growing up. He was the one person that I wanted to please more than anyone else in the world. I wanted to walk like him, talk like him, look like him and have the respect of the people like him. My father often took me and my two brothers with him on errands. I loved those times because I got to see how he related to people and how people related to him, and that's what I wanted. I was proud to be called LG Harrison's boy. He had a way of communicating that was firm, yet effective, and seasoned with grace. His style earned him respect from other adults and children alike. Throughout my childhood my father instilled plenty of life lesson's that helped cultivate my desire to be an effective leader.

My father taught me how to play and survive within the lines of reason. His presence alone commanded attention and respect. He was tall in stature, with a booming voice, and demeanor that let everyone know how protective he was of his family. Growing up in a time when it would have been easy to abandon his lot, he helped my mother raise 11 children all the while giving each of us quality time. For this, my dad has always been my hero. One of the main reasons I went to college was to make him proud. He instilled in all of us a sense of pride for our family name and honor for our parents and forefathers.

I clearly remember the time when I had the opportunity to try out for Meadowlark Lemon's Shooting Stars comedy basketball team. There was a typo in my stats that claimed I was 6'9 instead of 5'9. When the team's management learned about the error, they began to rethink their decision to bring me on board. On top of that, I had severely cut my finger 2 days before tryouts. I had two obstacles fighting against me, and I was losing the battle. The night before I was to leave, I was talking to my father about it. I told him that things did not look too good, and I was thinking about pulling out. The other end of the phone fell silent. It was only for a few seconds, but felt like an eternity. My dad then proceeded to remind me of all the hours that we had spent sweating in the gym. The snow days, hot days, and rainy days did not stop us then, so why should this situation stop me now? He advised me to go down there and do what I did best because nobody could beat me, being me. Those words of advice were like fire in my veins and I stuck in there, and was glad that I did.

Even so, there were other instances when his lessons were learned the hard way. It was back to school week. For the first time, my older brother, Richard, and younger brother, Maurice, and I got to go shopping at Richman Gordman's department store for our school shoes. We were excited because this was the first time we were allowed to shop alone. Our father entrusted us to follow his directives by completing the task responsibly; the way he had taught us.

After gazing longingly over the top of the line Chuck Taylors in the sneaker section, we headed for the cheap knock offs called Tuffy's. My brothers found their selections right away, but I was having the toughest time finding my size 8 ½. Because it was the first day of school, and I wanted to look my best, I ended up settling for a pair of size eights, which were really too tight. Despite the fit, I decided that I was not going to school without new shoes. We went home knowing that we had to share our purchases with our father for an inspection. Did I fail to mention that he was a gunnery sergeant in the Marines who was known for inspections?

After putting on our shoes, we proceeded to stroll back and forth before him so that he could check the fit. My brothers passed with flying colors. I, on the other hand, knew he would notice my bunched toes, not to mention awkward limp. My heart sank because I knew if he noticed that the fit was incorrect, I would be in trouble, or worse be made to wear my old shoes. When it was my turn to walk, I hobbled along, smiling as if everything was good. He noticed my off balanced stride, looked at me strangely, and asked if my feet hurt. Of course I said that the shoes felt fine. With some reluctance, he gave me a passing grade, and I went to my room to lay out my clothes for the big day feeling like I had won the lottery.

The next morning I woke up excited about the first day of school. After washing up, we ran to put on our clothes. When I opened the box to my new shoes, my heart fell at what I saw. My father had done the unthinkable. To teach me a lesson about not following directions, he had cut the toes out! To top it all off, he made me wear them! I couldn't get out of going to school because it was the first day. Despite my protest, I got into the car with my brothers and cried all the way to school.

When we arrived, my brothers jumped out of the car to meet their friends, but I wouldn't budge. In a calm voice, my father told me to go on to school, but I just could not do it. We went to an inner-city school where teasing was big. I didn't want to get teased or "crowed on" as we called it, on the first day. Seeing how upset I was, in a quiet voice my father asked me why I did not tell him that the shoes were too small. Had I communicated this to him, we could have gone to another store and found the shoes that I needed. We could have avoided the situation all together, had I been straight with him from the beginning.

He then got out of the car and went around to the trunk. I closed my eyes, thinking this was it. I was going to get a whipping now. Instead of a belt in his hand, imagine my surprise when he returned with another pair of shoes. While we were sleeping, he had gone out and bought me a pair that fit, and they were cooler than the ones I had. I was so happy! From that point on, I understood the importance of following instructions and communicating even if the news isn't so good.

As you know how boys are, I completely forgot all about this lesson when I was presented with another test. Once again, my brothers and I were given another opportunity to show how responsible we could be. We were asked to go to the neighborhood store to buy some breakfast cereal. All the way to the store, cereal was on our minds until we got there and saw that red box of Bugle corn chips. They were a newly introduced snack chip and the commercial on television promised that if you blew into a Bugle corn chip, it would

7

make the sound of a horn. Our curiosity to find out if this was true enticed us. Because they looked more like cereal than chips, we thought that our dad wouldn't notice the difference. My brothers and I went round and round about buying the Bugles versus the Cornflakes. Doing the right thing versus fulfilling our curiosity. Since Richard was the oldest, I concluded that if we got the Bugles, and our plan failed, he would have to take the heat. As I'm sure you know, our curiosity won out.

On the walk home, the three of us pretended like we weren't nervous by filling the air with empty talk all the while secretly waiting for the chance to blow into one of those tiny horns. When we got home, we were relieved to learn that our father had stepped out, and we had escaped the 1st line of inspection and were allowed to go outside to play. Soon after my father returned home, he called us inside to eat. There sat three bowls full of Bugles next to a gallon of milk ready to pour. Reluctantly, we took our seats as he poured the milk, then instructed us to eat, before leaving the room.

The Bugles were disgusting! The milk had practically melted them down to a soggy mess. We poured so much sugar on them in an effort to offset the saltiness, but it only made it worse. We even tried to feed it to our dog who had sense enough to walk away. After a few moments, my father returned to the kitchen and asked if we were full because we hadn't finished eating. The three of us looked at each other, but said nothing. In his usual infinite wisdom, he proceeded to tell us that we should not follow behind others especially when we know they are doing wrong. Following instructions is always the best way. Both lessons stayed with me to the point that whenever my father presented me with a task, I remembered those shoes and the Bugles and followed through.

Shirley Harrison (My Mom)

"Listen to what people don't say;
it's usually louder then what they do say"

My mother exemplified the very essence of a chaste, strong, understanding and loving woman. She equipped me with values and a level of respect for others as well as an ability to meet people where they are. She never told me what not to do, but guided me in a way that allowed me to always make the right decisions. There were three monumental occasions that taught me lessons that I hold onto this day.

It was January of my senior year and we were playing Tech High School at the University of Nebraska in Omaha. Our teams were inner-city rivals, and the match up put me against my good friends and cousins. This was a game that was cancelled earlier in the year due to inclement weather, but the Tech players jokingly said it was so we could get my friend Big Nasty eligible to play.

The game was intense from the start. There was a lot of trash talking, and my cousin Calvin was doing the majority of it. I got tired of his comments and decided to just *beast* him by posting him up and dominating in the paint, which I knew I could do. I kept asking for the ball, but I was getting overlooked. Anger rose in me because I wanted to make Calvin pay for his words. After being open for what seemed like the hundredth time, I finally yelled out, "Pass me the mother F-ing ball!" When I realized what I said, I looked over at my mother. Her expression was that of shock and embarrassment. When she lowered her head, I immediately felt ashamed. Though she never said a word to me afterwards, her actions spoke volumes, and I never said a curse word again in my life.

The next time was during the spring of my senior year. All the fellas were playing basketball at Bryant Center, a local basketball court. Bryant Center drew all of the top inner city players. It was a place where reputations were made, and in some cases destroyed. My plans involved getting home, changing, grabbing a bite to eat and hitting the courts. On this particular day, however, my mother had other plans for me. She needed me to stay at home and help out with my younger siblings since my father was out of town. I didn't want to do that, so I elected to go play ball any way. Bad move. When I returned home that evening, all of my clothes were thrown out on the back lawn. I tried going inside, but my mother wouldn't unlock the door. Instead, she advised that I stay with the people that were so important to play basketball with earlier that day. That was the second time that I really felt like I let her down. It was the worst feeling in the world.

Because she wouldn't let me in the house, I decided that I was going to show her. I headed straight for this Air Force recruiter's house to see about enlisting. It was 9:30 at night, but I didn't care. I should have known that something was up when Sergeant Mc Swain came to the door in a robe and carrying a wine glass. A glance over his shoulder revealed his wife, also robed, on the floor with a wine glass in her hand. The mood was set for love with Barry White crooning in the background, and I knew I wasn't going to be staying there.

So, I did the only thing I could think to do, and that was go back home to make amends with my mother. She was calmer when I arrived as she actually opened the door. When I agreed to never disrespect or hurt her again, she relented but with a straight face calmly warned me, "Don't let it happen again. Now get your clothes off the ground before it rains." Got to love her.

The third episode occurred while I was a young adult in Salem, Oregon, living in an apartment with practically no furniture. All I had was a couch and a T.V. One day, a friend called to ask me if I wanted to buy a VCR for $60. That was a great deal in those days especially when a brand new VCR could cost upwards of $300. I decided right then and there that I wanted it. Because it was so cheap, I knew that it had to be stolen, but I didn't care. Before my friend brought it over, I called my mother to share my good fortune. In her usual calm voice she warned, "If you get it, you can never be mad if someone steals something from you. You are keeping the thief in business, and better yet, he knows where to come and steal a VCR if someone wants one." Man those words so resonated within me that I called my friend, and told him I changed my mind. From those life lesson's I take pride in doing the right thing and never bring embarrassment to my family, city or country.

At the end of the day, the most overwhelming key to a child's success is the positive involvement of parents.
~Jane D. Hull

The Ball Is In Your Court

During my travels, speaking to youth around the world, I have learned that many children come from households where the traditional concept of family has changed. The role of mother, father, brother, sister or grandparent, for that matter and the responsibilities typically associated with them, no longer exist. Because of this, the guidance or care that children receive today may not necessarily come from a nurturing place.

It is paramount that we take the role of mentor or role model seriously. Young people look up to those closest to them. They want and need love, attention and affirmation. They are impressionable too. They soak up everything like sponges, good or bad. News and magazine articles often talk negatively about the next generation. This was first seen after World War II with the population boom in the United States. There are the Baby Boomers, Generation X, Generation Y, Generation Z and the latest Generation Alpha. Each one has a description with attached tags like "stuck" "slacker" "lazy" "techno minded" and "materialistic" without the generation before taking some sort of responsibility.

It's time to be accountable for the next generation. Spend some time, impart knowledge, teach a new skill, or lend a listening ear. Let's get rid of the negative tags marking our youth, and start applying words like "success" "promise" and "generous." If we do so, we can change the world.

TEACHING

Do not train children to learning by force and harshness,
but direct them to it by what amuses their minds, so that you may
be better able to discover with accuracy the peculiar bent
of the genius of each.
~Plato

Many think that a great teacher's effectiveness is measured by the academic progress of her students. Therefore, teachers who taught AP classes were considered to be superior because their students typically carried higher GPA's. On the other hand, teachers with students who did not perform well in the classroom, and had learning challenges or simply lacked resources, were considered inadequate.

Well, I did not pick up the art of traditional learning very well. AP courses were out of the question. Although I wasn't classified as Special Ed, I definitely qualified for some kind of services. Thank God, I had teachers in my life who took a special interest in me and wanted to go the extra mile to see that I learned what I needed at the moment to thrive. Too often teachers with low performing students are often overlooked. They do not receive the same accolades as their counterparts because awards do not come attached with their classes. I believe that successful teachers are those whose motives are in the right place. They love teaching, and are sincerely interested in a child's wellbeing. Great teaching takes patience, dedication and ingenuity to open up the most challenging child's mind.

Bobbie Kerrigan Rawley
"Find your laughter from within."

We had just transferred from a public school to Sacred Heart Elementary, an inner city Catholic school in our neighborhood. My brothers, sisters and I had attended the more racially diverse Central Grade School located in downtown Omaha for some time. While we lived in a predominantly African American neighborhood, the transfer of schools was still a great change for us.

Central Grade School, although a public school, was surprisingly laid back. The teachers were soft spoken, and the students were orderly, which contrasted against the private Catholic school setting at Sacred Heart. Sacred Heart reminded me of the many popular 70's sitcoms that I watched on television like *The White Shadow, Good Times* and *Welcome Back, Kotter* because of their colorful cast of characters.

Since we would be attending a school in our predominantly black neighborhood, I expected to be surrounded by black students and most likely black teachers. So, imagine my surprise when this beautiful, bubbly, blonde entered the room and introduced herself as our teacher, Bobbie Kerrigan. She was like Barbara Eden in *I Dream of Jeanie,* or at least she looked like her to me. She was young, barely out of college, yet optimistic and ready to make her mark in the lives of a group of inner city kids.

I struggled early in school, and although they were attentive, my former teachers didn't seem to require much out of me. At Sacred Heart, those days were over. Demands were placed on me to perform. Ms. Kerrigan was determined not to lose one student or even allow us to give up on ourselves. She took time building relationships with each kid and their families. She engaged us in and outside of the classroom and had an antidote for all of our crazy antics.

I was really struggling in school and was hoping to get lost in the shuffle. I must have had a target on my back that read 'in hiding' because Ms. Kerrigan seemed to zoom in on me like a lioness on prey. She had me figured out so well that when I got in trouble in other classes, they would send me to her class to finish my work.

The only outlet we had at Sacred Heart was kick ball, football in the lot behind the school, and basketball with the school garbage can for a basket. This school had very limited resources so we made do with what we had, which was one kick ball that doubled as a basketball *and* football. Then one day a miracle descended upon us and we got footballs, red, white and blue basketballs, baseball equipment and a Frisbee. Ms. Kerrigan got us to play football with a football, basketball with a basketball (albeit still in a garbage can) and so on. She got us so involved that soon we were playing other schools in flag football. We even went to the park with her family and friends to play Frisbee. She would get a group of her friends together to transport us to parks with actual grass! We were seeing parts of the city that we didn't know existed. She instilled a sense of pride in us by opening up our minds to new experiences.

It was during my time in Ms. Kerrigan's class that I discovered a gift in me. It was a natural ability to make others laugh. I didn't consider myself to be a funny kid, but it was that tiny spark in her eye, coupled by my desire to please, that fanned the flames to my future in entertainment.

I was on my way to school, debating if I should try to beat the tardy bell, or make a detour to the corner store to buy a Hostess apple pie. I had been dreaming about that pie all night after I saw a commercial on television, and just had to have one. At the last minute, I decided to take my chances, and ran the back route to the store. After making my purchase, I ran all the way to school, wolfing down that pie at the same time. By the time I got to school, the bell had rung, and I needed a note to get into class. If I didn't present a tardy note, it would mean a call home and punishment from my father. So, I got this brilliant idea to forge a note. I sat on the steps of the school and begin composing my own tardy excuse.

The note went something like this.

> *Please let Leslie in class. I'm dying, and*
> *I needed his help today.*
> *Signed Leslie's Mother*

I thought the letter was pretty good considering I had never seen my mother's signature on anything. With evidence (crumbs) on my face, I walked in the class and handed the note to Ms. Kerrigan. Despite the content, I noticed the spark in her eye and the slight smile she fought to hold back. There's no doubt that she questioned the note's authenticity, but she never said anything to me about it. However, years later as an adult, I learned that she had talked to my mother, but they were so entertained by my creativity that I didn't get into trouble.

I couldn't get the image of that spark in Ms. Kerrigan's eyes out of my head. I enjoyed how she responded and wanted to test this comedy realm a little further, and I did. About a week later, she had stepped outside of the classroom to talk with a teacher while the class watched a film. The second she left the room, the class began talking. She popped her head back inside and firmly warned, "Less talking and more listening." Being the kids that we were, the minute she stepped back out, we started talking again. This time she when poked her head in the room, her eyes landed on me. In stern teacher form, she asked the proverbial question, "What did I just say?" Right then, I knew it was my moment to shine. I calmly replied, "You said, Les talk and more listen." Well that did it. The class laughed and she joined in, although I knew she didn't approve of my off humor. Now I knew I had her. So, the next time I came prepared.

The night before, I had watched the Carol Burnett show and a skit with Tim Conway portraying a flasher. In the skit, Conway wore a trench coat and whenever he got in front of women he would open it up and shout "ooh-wah!" The next day, I wore my trench coat to school (with clothes on of course). I knew there was going to be a time when she would call me out for doing something, and I was going to be prepared. Like clockwork she called me to her desk for some reason or another. As I stood in front of her, she asked if I was cold because I was wearing a coat indoors. Instead of replying, I simply opened my coat and said, "ooh-wah!" Her face turned red and she got up and left the room, trying not to laugh. She couldn't return with a straight face and stood outside for several minutes. I knew then and there that I wanted to make people laugh.

Around that time, I began to show an interest in playing basketball. I really enjoyed the game but wasn't the best player. Whenever I made a mistake, I turned a potentially embarrassing situation into a comedic one to relieve the embarrassment and tension. It was then that Ms. Kerrigan began talking to me about the Harlem Globetrotters and how one day I could become one. I remember her even having teachers come to the gym to watch me handle the ball. The more they enjoyed it, the more I performed. Thank you, Bobbie (Kerrigan) Rawley for seeing past my antics, and introducing me to entertainment by speaking to life those things that were not, as if they were.

Mr. Paul Bangura

"Don't get stabbed in your belly with your back turned."

Creighton Prep was like the Notre Dame of high schools in Omaha. While they were strong academically, it was the basketball program that drew my attention. Prep had a pretty good team with diehard fans. I enjoyed watching the fans as much as the games. Their Pep Club with their blue and white painted faces, staged bleacher acts, and rowdy cheers were entertaining in itself. While I was in my element at the games, the classroom was a different story.

I had a hard time getting decent grades in all of my classes, but I really struggled in Mr. Bangura's biology class. Biology was the class where I could not get over. Because of this, I did whatever I could to pass. I copied homework notes, made friends with the book worms, even tried to cheat on my tests just to get a "D". The only reason why I went through all of these measures is because I needed this class to be eligible to play basketball. Needless to say by the second week, I knew my basketball career wouldn't be at Prep if it meant passing Mr. Bangura's class. My mind began to go into overdrive to come up with some kind of way to score a passing grade. I began to employ tactics such as befriending him, comedy, or just plain hoping that he was a die-hard sports (particularly basketball) fan and that he would love to see me bring my show to The Bird Cage (Prep's gym).

Just when I thought I had Mr. Bangura in the bag, I quickly realized that he had me. All of my plans backfired when I learned Mr. Bangura was from Africa, and that the student teacher relationship is not like that of the United States. In his country, students regarded their teachers with a high degree of honor. Their relationship was one of mutual respect and decency, so my attempts at comedy were not well received. My hope that he'd be a basketball fan failed too because he wasn't into the sport at all. In fact he was the varsity soccer coach. After many failed attempts to take the easy road, he asked me to step out in the hallway. With a grim expression on his face, he simply said, "Mr. Harrison, you have been demonstrating very poor academic prowess. Did you think all you had to do was smile and bounce a basketball to pass my class? If so, you are sadly mistaken."

Wow! Talk about some heavy words to hear. While I don't believe Mr. Bangura was trying to insult me, I do believe he saw something more than what I was willing to show him. It was right then that I learned that I needed a solid foundation to build upon. I wasted a whole quarter *faking the funk* when it would have been a whole lot easier taking the time to learn each concept presented before me. While Mr. Bangura gave it to me straight, I learned to smile even when the news wasn't so good. So, when I say, "don't get stabbed in your belly with your back turned," what I mean is that the only way a person can stab you in your belly while your back is turned, is if they are close to you. The closest person to me, at the time, who knew about my short comings was me.

The Ball Is In Your Court

Did you realize that as a whole, children spend most of their waking time in an organized setting under the care of a teacher? That equals to 40 hours a week, 160 hours a month, and 2080 hours a year. If you subtract that 8 hours from a child's 24-hour day, factoring in 8 hours of sleep time, that leaves 8 hours to split between homework, workouts, sporting events etc. That is a lot of time to make a significant difference in a child's life. When I was in school, education was taught in a traditional manner. There wasn't much variation. We were taught our time tables by rote memorization. We learned cursive writing during penmanship sessions and new words were introduced phonetically. Times have changed. There are more distractions in a child's life. They have the world at their fingertips through computers with Internet which they can tap into on a device as small as a cell phone. Not to mention social media, video games and the like. There is a lot competing for young people's time and attention. Individuals working with children must be more innovative in their approach while at the same time daring to see past all of the challenges children face by recognizing the light glimmering inside his heart and mind. When you do, you'll be tapping into the heartbeat of their destiny.

"The mediocre teacher tells. The good teacher explains. The superior teacher demonstrates. The great teacher inspires."
~William Arthur Ward

FRIENDSHIP

*"There is a magnet in your heart that will attract true friends.
That magnet is unselfishness, thinking of others first;
when you learn to live for others, they will live for you."*
~ *Paramahansa Yogananda*

A friendship is a type of relationship between two people who care about each other. But such a dry definition does not do the concept of friendship justice. Consider these examples: A friend is the first person you want to call when you hear good news. A friend remembers that you like ketchup on everything. A friend will accompany you on the most boring of errands and make them seem fun.

According to researchers,

*In a lifetime, one makes 396 friendships but only one in 12, (33) stands the test of time.

*Out of the 33, only 6 are considered to be close friends while the 27 are social friends i.e. workmates or drinking buddies.

*Best friends are not those one sees most often but those one thinks of most.

In other words, friendship is wonderful, and much ink has been spilled in citing the virtues of having friends. That's not to say friendship is easy, though. It demands time and effort, and it requires that people put someone other than themselves first sometimes. But in exchange for that work, a friend can provide an immense amount of support and comfort in good times and in bad. I have been fortunate to have some wonderful people in my life as friends. They have walked with me through the good times and the not so good. Because they have made such an indelible impression in my heart, I must recognize their contribution in my life.

Milton McBride a.k.a Big Nasty

"Friendship is a two way street."

The year was 1980 and the location was Central High School. After transferring from Creighton Prep, I found myself feeling like a stranger in a strange land. Unlike Prep, Central had a student body of more than 1500 students. Plus, it had a lot of girls, not to mention the fact that it was more racially diverse. Creighton Prep, on the other hand, had an all-male student body of about 600 with only 10 being students of color.

When I arrived at Central with the intent of playing basketball, the word was already out that a transfer from Prep was there, and the players wanted to see what I was all about. One of those players was this 6'5, 220 pound guy named Milton McBride. Milton sported one of the biggest afros that I had ever seen in person. He was very charismatic and confident, and was deemed as the unofficial spokesman for the Central men's basketball team. Right off, he was very aggressive about obtaining my stats as well as my personal information. My immediate thought was, great, this varsity player is trying to haze me. This guy is looking for trouble and most likely going to be a headache the whole year and that's not what I wanted or needed at a new school.

After my interrogation by Milton the "mayor" of the team, we went to practice. The Varsity and JV teams practiced in one gym and sophomores in another. Because I hadn't been assigned to either team, I was on the same court as Milton. I made a mental note to stay out of his way.

We were all assembled in the main gym before splitting off into our respective teams. Keep in mind, I was a middle-of-the-season transfer, and the teams had already been formed. It was a rarity that any coach would take on a new player especially after there had been cuts and teams established. Out of the corner of my eye, I noticed Milton's big afro bopping around performing his mayoral duties amongst his followers and supporters. When the whistle blew and we were instructed to go to our separate courts, instead of staying with me, "the afro" left the gym. I was baffled, and resolved that maybe Coach sent him over to work with the younger guys. Come to find out, he *was* one of the younger guys who played on the sophomore team! I, for some strange reason, remained with the JV and Varsity teams. Man I was excited for 2 reasons, one I was at least placed on the JV team, and two, I didn't have to deal with Milton.

The next morning at school, I was by myself on the stairs looking down into the main area called 'the hump' where the cool kids gathered every morning. Once again, out of the corner of my eye, I spotted that big afro, and right on his heels were his followers. Now Milton was always surrounded by the cool guys and pretty girls. I watched him maneuver around with confidence, and in many ways I admired the respect he received. I didn't have any guys or girls around me like him. Keep in mind that I came from and all boys' school, and the only girls I had come in contact with were at home, and they were my six sisters.

Standing on those stairs, I made up my mind that he was out of my league. Right at that moment, Milton glanced up and saw me on the stairs by myself. I must have looked very much out of place and alone like an open target. Before I knew it, he was heading my way followed by an entourage of football players. Man, I didn't know what to expect. I was nervous, trying to think about what I should do or say if he said something off color to me. So, imagine my surprise when all he wanted to do was introduce me to the guys. We all hung out there until first period started and for the first time, I felt like I belonged at Central. When it was all said and done it was pretty cool. Each day, Milton kept showing up and introducing me to new people, sitting with me at lunch with his partners, and even supporting me at the games. Our friendship grew and I looked forward to hanging out with him. This guy socialized me and did what no one else had ever done. He befriended me. He made my two and a half years at Central the best days of my high school life. He became a part of my family and to this very day is considered my best friend. The acts of kindness that he demonstrated towards me, I employ in my life today. I make sure I speak to people I don't know, and I always pick out people who appear to be lonely or in need of friends. Professionally, I centered my business on helping youth around the world through a character education program with a core message of friendship and being a friend.

Did I mention that Milton, aka "Big Nasty" is the main character in my program? I gave him that name by the end of our sophomore year because he was big and he used to think that his moves on the court were so sweet, while I used to say, "Man those moves are nasty." Nasty didn't mean good back then, nasty meant ugly. Thanks Big Nasty for showing me the selflessness of a real friendship.

Cornelius Williams

"Be a great target."

I first heard about Cornelius Williams during my rookie year while playing with Meadowlark Lemon's Shooting Stars. I had called up my former teammate Curtis Kimbrough, who was still playing at George Fox College, to catch up on lost time when he began telling me about this new player in the league named Cornelius Williams. Curtis boasted about this guy who played like Dominique Wilkins, and could dunk on anybody. When we had a break in our tour, I couldn't wait to see this guy everyone was talking about, but when I went home, our paths never crossed. Unfortunately, I never got the chance to see him play that year, but the opportunity presented itself in all places in the world—the Lancaster Mall in Salem, Oregon.

At the time, I was visiting my then girlfriend, Rachel, who worked at the mall when I heard this loud voice echoing down the hall. Bounding in my direction was this 6'2 black guy wearing a tight t-shirt with cut off sleeves, and a Kangol hat looking like LL Cool Jay, a popular rapper. He was surrounded by a flock of people and I immediately wondered who he was. He appeared to be very sure of himself with a slight resemblance to Will Smith, charisma of Bill Clinton, and the humorous edge of comedian Bernie Mac. Although we didn't meet that day, he did stay in my mind.

My next encounter with Cornelius wasn't until we played on a city league team put together by a mutual friend. He was every bit the player that everyone said he was, but I deemed him as having an unusual style of play. He was a dominating player who expended more energy than needed. His teammates were more captivated by his game that they did not know how to work with him. Yes, we won games because we were a very talented team. However, we all were not reaching our full potential with his style of play. I knew that as the point guard, I had to do something.

One day, I decided that I would avoid passing him the ball as much in order to give others a chance to be involved in the game. I understood that in the long run we would need everyone's participation when the competition got tougher. Well, we really bumped heads over the change that he knew nothing about. I started to hear and see his frustration as well as that of my other team mates. I knew we had to make some changes before we killed each other and everyone around us. So, I had to take another approach and decided to take the time to talk with him. I wanted him to understand what I saw on the court and how we could better work together. Well, that talk did not go well, but I was determined to not give up.

Cornelius and I played as many as 100 games together and all the while, I was looking for opportunities to talk with him. Finally, the open door came when both he and I moved into a trailer (affectionately called the condo) in the driveway of his former coach's house. Neither one of us had two nickels to rub between us. Our days were built around our survival with meager resources. We would play basketball during the day, shower at Chemeketa Community College, and then play city league at night all before making our daily 11:00 pm Dunkin Donut runs to buy a dozen of donuts for $1.50 for breakfast the next morning.

Well this particular night I took a chance to talk to him. I began by expressing how good of a player he was, and that I believed he could be a lot better if I could get the ball to him so that he didn't have to work as hard. I set up a system where he could have success with half the effort. It took some time working out the details but soon we developed a trust and oneness of mind. After that, we became unstoppable no matter who we played against. He was the perfect target and made my job a lot easier, which really pressed me to simplify the game; therefore, bringing out a level of enjoyment that I relish to this day. There was John Stockton and Karl Malone, Magic and Kareem, Michael and Scottie then there was Les and Corn. I wouldn't pick any other person to go to battle with.

We became so dominate that those who played around us soon adopted our style of play and we became the dynamic duo of the Northwest. We scored 200 points twice in games and averaged about 150 points per game over the next 3 years. We also won every tournament you could win in the Northwest. From Pro-Am to money tournaments, and 3 on 3, all I needed was my target, and no one has perfected positioning in order to succeed more than my brother-in-law Cornelius Williams. When two people work together and are on one accord, it's amazing at what they can accomplish.

Curly Neal

"Just make them smile"

The first session of training camp was over, and all of the players were headed back to their condominiums. It was a very beautiful day in sunny Southern California. Because I did not have a place to stay, and hadn't made any friends, I wasn't in a hurry to go anywhere. As I slowly, got my things together, I could overhear the returning players rambled on about the rookies they liked and those they were not particularly impressed with.

While I was engrossed in their banter, something near the pool caught my attention. I moved to get a better view in time to see this man, surrounded by a group of people. He was not an ordinary man, but one who was spotless and without wrinkle; every bit the Hollywood type, if I said so myself. He was dressed in all white, with a matching brimmed hat, and his sparkling smile shone as brightly as the thick gold necklace around his neck. Who was this guy? I thought while wondering which movie set he was on his way to.

When the crowd dissipated, I realized that the guy with the infectious smile was none other than Curly Neal himself. I couldn't believe that the Globetrotter who was known for his ball handling skills on the floor was actually here! The other team members rose to hug and give him high fives. I was surprised when he walked around and acknowledged everyone, including me. I thought that was pretty cool, being that the other "stars" were more standoffish.

As pre-season started I got to know the players up close and personal. There was something that really stood out about Curly more so than the others. He had to be the most famous bald basketball player at that time in the history of the world. In fact he was just as recognizable because of his bald head as he was in the blue jersey and red and white striped shorts. During those days it was more popular for Black men to wear afros and Jheri curls, but not Curly. He was different. He was his own person, choosing not to buy into what everyone else was doing, but walking his own path.

He was a humble guy who never sought attention for himself, but would always take a back seat and would only chime in to support those around him. He was like that on the court as well. In games, Curly played the backup role to Meadowlark. He could have done what many of the other players would do to gain attention and increase his popularity, but he never relished in that limelight. He was the best second banana (supporting cast member) to play the game. He allowed Batman, The Green Hornet, and Meadowlark to get all the accolades. He understood that his role was to make sure Meadowlark was at his best, and that he had to be at his best in order to make that happen. Talk about the original Boy Wonder!

Curly taught me how to stay humble on the court and when to use charisma to get the job done. He recognized that I had *it* and he taught me how to use *it* at the proper time and place. Therefore, I learned when to smile, when to give a kid a hug and when to step into the shadows. He taught me how to stand and move on the court in a fashion that would only add to what Meadowlark was doing. Curly showed me the importance of servant leadership. He was devoted to the bigger picture, which was entertaining the fans and he didn't have to be the center of attention to get that done.

Over the next 25 years I was amazed at his devotion to the role of second banana as well as to the fans. He would never leave the gym until he signed autographs for all who wanted one. There were games that we played without Meadowlark and he allowed me to be *first banana* while he played his normal role. Curly always elevated others higher then himself. This mind frame and thought process I continue to carry with me on and off the court to this day. Always esteem others more highly then yourself. To watch Curly perform his tricks on the court without saying a word was truly admiring an artist and a great servant at work.

I think if I've learned anything about friendship,
it's to hang in, stay connected, fight for them, and let
them fight for you. Friends are part of the glue that
holds life and faith together. Powerful stuff.
~ Jon Katz

The Ball Is In Your Court

I have two thoughts that I would like to say about friendship.

#1. Never underestimate the power of a true friendship.
#2. Never reject the possibility of a new friendship.

From the time we come into the world, we connect with our parents or caregivers. When babies grow into preschoolers, they form relationships with people outside of their family in school settings. Those friendships may last or fade away due to outside or societal influences.

When people get caught up in the thought that they can only have endearing friendships with people on their economic or social level, who live in their immediate community or attend their worship services and happen to look, act or think like them, they are cutting off an opportunity to have an awesome life experience.

Friendship, like anything, takes work. What we put in is what we will get back. I often tell people that we can't put our view of friendship on others and expect them to reciprocate the way we want. Friendship is about accepting people where they are and learning to appreciate different trains of thought and culture. Accepting where one is at a particular stage in life is the most important element in any relationship because you are starting at a point of understanding. Seek to understand before being understood. I never met a man that I didn't like. Every friend that I've made from day one, I still consider them a friend until this day.

LEADERSHIP

"Sports creates a bond between contemporaries that lasts a lifetime. It also gives your life structure, discipline and a genuine, sincere, pure fulfillment that few other areas of endeavor provide."
~Bob Cousy

When one hears the word leader, many meanings come to mind depending on the hearer. In a child's mind it could be the first one in line in a playground game. To a misguided youth running the streets, a leader can be the mastermind behind a street gang. In the community, a leader can be one who heads up an honorable cause. And in the business world, the leader can be defined by others as one who runs a successful corporation, has a sizeable bank account, or who manages a large number of people. In each of these examples, the position of the leader was purposeful. I like the definition of a leader in John Haggai's book, *The Influential Leader.* He says that around the world there are millions of people in leadership positions, but very few qualify as being *influential leaders.* An influential leaders are "Leaders who use their influence to transform the world around them and leave a lasting impact for good." The key words that stand out to me most are "transform the world" and "lasting impact." Leaders typically do not accept the title without attempting to make a difference whether good or bad.

I was fortunate to have good examples of leaders in my life who made an impact in my thinking, and how I relate to others as a leader. Haggai's says that the one dominant character trait that influential leaders have is a particular way of making decisions. My coaches, Jim Martin, Dan Johnson, Mark Vernon and Meadowlark Lemon taught me great life lessons on how to be effective as a leader both personally and professionally while making an indelible impression in the lives of others.

Jim Martin

"Don't Take Things for Granted"

In 9th grade, I followed in my older brother Richard's steps by attending Creighton Prep High School. Little did my brother know that he was my idol. I wanted to be just like him. He was smart, athletic and tall, a near perfect candidate to play basketball. There was no other school that I wanted to attend except Creighton Prep. For one, they had a solid sports program, which had produced some great athletes. They were also strong academically, graduating some of Nebraska's top scholars. In addition, I wanted to keep with the Harrison family private school tradition.

Upon, graduating from Sacred Heart, I immediately registered at Creighton Prep. Education was one of the Harrison's cherished family values and because Creighton Prep was a college preparatory school, my father thought it would make me a shoe in for a college scholarship. I looked forward to walking the halls with my classmates, proudly displaying my Blue Jay insignia. However, my enthusiasm was short lived when I quickly realized that Prep's challenging curriculum was well—a challenge. As a result, I barely squeaked by during my freshman year.

By December of my sophomore year, my grades were still not what they needed to be to remain a student at Prep. Due to academic struggles, I had no choice but to transfer to another school. I was pretty upset about this because I really wanted to play basketball with my brother and cousins. Despite my objections, the next semester, my father transferred me to Omaha Central High School.

Central was also a school rich in academics and sports traditions, having players on its rosters such as sports figures Gale Sayers of the Chicago Bears, Larry Station of the Pittsburgh Steelers and Ahman Green of the Green Bay Packers as well as notable actors like Henry Fonda and Dorothy McGuire. When I learned that some pretty famous people had once walked Central's halls, I resolved that this would be my new school.

Because I transferred during the Christmas break, the

basketball teams had already been formed. I thought I would have to wait until the following year to play. This was nothing new since I had already missed playing ball my freshman year and half of my sophomore year due to academic and physical injury sustained while at Prep. I was surprised to be picked for any team, Junior Varsity at that.

On the first day of practice, I was approached by fellow player, Milton McBride. He said that he had heard I was pretty good, and could throw crazy assists as if challenging me to show him something. I simply replied, that he had to wait like everyone else to find out. His approach made me realize that people were expecting me to have talent, and if all eyes were on me, I was obligated to not let them down.

I was able to demonstrate my skills at the first practice, and during my first year earned a reputation as a great passer and defensive juggernaut. I loved the "oohs" and "ahs" when I threw a complicated pass that helped our team to score. I felt like I had found my calling card. Passing, also known as assisting, was really big during that time because of greats like Magic Johnson who was regarded as the best. I wanted to show everyone that I was the best passer—period.

The following year, I moved up to the Varsity team under Coach Martin. I was driven by the possibility of continuing my assist and defensive show, but on a grander stage, the varsity level. Jim Martin was considered to be one of the best coaches in the state, having a couple State Championships under his belt before I arrived at Central. Not only had he won state titles, but he was also known for taking his players' game to the next level. But this year would be different. The team was in their rebuilding stage after having lost all of the seniors to graduation and the like. Right away I knew that redeeming the glory days would be an uphill battle.

We didn't have the size or the skills to compete with the majority of the other schools. We did experience some highs, but we also had our share of lows, and boy were there many. I wanted to be on a winning team so bad that I tried everything to make us better. I helped Coach choose the starting lineup and even went as far as to try and design the teams' uniforms! I was practically running the show, in my mind. The whole time, Coach Martin watched and waited. It was then that he taught me the meaning of the word "granted." He told me that I was taking it for granted that I would make the varsity team. Rather, than focus on my next move, I needed to focus on staying on the team as no spot was guaranteed.

Integrity ranked high on Coach's list when it came to his players and the game itself. He won a lot of games with integrity and gained respect from not only his team, but opposing teams as well. He showed me that my efforts to improve the team were fruitless because I was more concerned about being the best instead of being the best leader. He taught us how to be gracious when losing games while maintaining respect for the game in the process. He demanded more leadership out of me in a losing situation than he did out of his point guards on his winning teams. He taught me how to effectively communicate on the floor with him and my team mates with respect. During every timeout or stop of play, I would always go over to Coach Martin and consult with him on the teams' status, where we wanted to be by a certain point in the game, and how we were all going to get there together. He would never have to yell at us because we were in constant communication. Needless to say, my 2 years on the team, under Coach's leadership, drastically improved my strategic thinking and direct communication skills.

At the end of the season, Coach Martin told me not to take the lessons that I learned over the past 2 ½ years for granted because they formed character and leadership in me that I would be able to use for the rest of my life. In 2013 I gave Coach Martin the greatest accomplishment that one could give a coach. I was the first basketball player to be inducted into the Hall of Fame at Central, and I shared how Coach Martin assisted me on becoming the man I am today.

Dan Johnson

"Always make sure the juice is worth the squeeze"

Dan Johnson was my first college coach at Iowa Western Community College in Clarinda Iowa. Before I transferred to IWCC, I was a student at Langston University in Langston, Oklahoma. I had been in communication with the coach and he agreed to let me come and tryout for the team. When I arrived on campus, I was surprised to learn that he was fired and had been replaced by a new coach.

Prior to arriving on campus, I had suffered a broken wrist and was in a cast. The new coach, who took his place, was not interested in me trying out with a broken wrist, and told me to wait until next year. Well that was not the answer I needed to hear, nor wanted to for that matter. All I could do was pack my bags and head back to Omaha, but there was another plan in store. My good friend, Alex Murphy was leaving to attend school at Iowa Western Community College in Clarinda, Iowa. He suggested that I go with him. Because I had nowhere else to go, I agreed. He picked me up and we were off for Clarinda.

Alex tossed me a perfect assist when he walked me through the admissions process and pulled some strings to get me on the team even though my arm was still in a cast. A week after enrollment, we went back to Omaha to get my cast removed. Boy was I ready, or so I thought. My wrist was weak and it hurt at the slightest touch. I feared being rejected again by the new coach and momentarily watched my college dreams of playing basketball fade before my eyes. Thank God Alex had a different perspective.

He had me workout with him before and after practice. His workouts were tougher than any workouts I had ever done. He was hard on me, but I needed it. By the end of 2 ½ weeks, my wrist was in shape enough to join the team and practices. While I gave what I thought was my best effort, I ended up being the 13th guy on the team. All the other players had worked hard to establish the rotation, and I was not in it. Coach Johnson didn't even acknowledge me. I resigned to the fact that I would just be a practice player who would never play in any real games. However, this changed when we were in a Thanksgiving tournament in Kansas City.

It was the championship game and we were beating the opposing team pretty bad from the 2ⁿᵈ quarter on. With 25 seconds left in the game, Coach Johnson does the unthinkable. He tells me to go in. I gave him a look, thinking surely he was kidding, but he wasn't. By the time I got in the game, it was basically over with only five seconds remaining on the clock. This was my most embarrassing basketball moment ever. I kept thinking that it would have been better if I hadn't played at all. Once we got back to the school, I packed my bags and left school. I decided that I would follow in my father's footsteps and join the Marines, vowing to never put up with that type of embarrassment again.

After completing paperwork to become one of the *few and the proud*, I was instructed to go for my physical. I was surprised when I discovered that the doctor who was performing my physical was the same doctor who delivered me and seven of my siblings. He proceeded to ask me about my family and if my father knew that I was enlisting into the military? With downcast eyes, I admitted that I kept it from him. He encouraged me to rethink what I was doing by talking with my father first. Apparently all was not lost. I had one more chance to change my mind about enlisting, and he told me exactly what I needed to do. I followed his advice, and my father, who never gives up, made me go back to IWCC.

This time when I went back, I had a strategy. I made up in my mind that since I wasn't getting any playing time in the game, I was going to do my thing in practice. I had nothing to lose. The first practice back, I dominated in the number of steals. I did the same thing at the next practice and the next. Before long, Coach Johnson had no choice but to notice me. At one practice he made a comment that fueled me. He said, "Who's guarding Les? You're making him look like a F-ing All American!" That's all I needed to hear to change my course. That was the greatest insult anyone could give me. Unbeknownst to him, Coach Johnson inspired me to look inside myself without outside help. His actions and words encouraged me to show myself and others that I had something to offer, I counted. The lesson that I learned from Alex Murphy, Coach Johnson, my Dad, and Dr. Margolin is that no matter what life throws at you, stay in the game. Each one of them, played a key role by passing the ball for a perfect shot. Before walking away from a tough situation, it was important to make sure the juice is worth the squeeze.

Mark Vernon

"You never know what you're missing until someone gives you something you never had."

Mark Vernon was my coach at George Fox University. He is no doubt the best coach that I've ever played for. His coaching style was like that of a fox—cool and calculating. He viewed coaching as a challenge and enjoyed outsmarting his opponents with his innovative style of playing the game. The approach he took was light years ahead of anyone I knew.

He had an uncanny ability to make all 5 starters on the team feel like they were the leader of the team. Most teams have one leader or captain, but Coach Vernon tacitly promoted each of us in the position, thereby giving us the freedom to do what we did best, which allowed us to shine. We all took pride in our contributions, which showed as we led the league in each statistical category, which put us on the national scene as well. We worked together as a fine tuned machine night in and night out. If he had to reprimand us, it would be for performing below level, which made us constantly aware of our game.

He was always coming up with simple things to make us look great. It was a very simple method. He broke the game down in segments where we all had a chance to shine and be stars.

Whenever Coach sat down to talk with me, he'd always say how vital it was for me to run the team. Without me leading the team, we would not have success. This made me feel like I was the glue that would lead us to a win. I later learned that he did the same with all of the other players. He told the leading scorer that we needed the buckets. He told the leading rebounder that he needed to secure loose balls and so on. He made each of us feel responsible for putting forth our best effort, to avoid a loss. We were like a smooth running machine with each of us playing a specific yet significant part.

His style created a unique level of trust amongst the team that I have never experienced before, or have seen since. Coach would have a saying when it came to making a mistake. He would say, "Good idea." This approach didn't take away our creativity, it actually enhanced it, which gave us a sense of invincibility. We looked forward to getting on the floor every night to do our thing and not let him down. None of us ever doubted that we were the leader of the team. Coach Vernon was a very forward thinker, and I believe all leaders must employ the train of thought.

Meadowlark Lemon
"Make it do what it do baby!"

It was September 1986, and I was at an LA Training camp with legends such as Pistol Pete Maravich, Curly Neal, Gator Rivers, Little John Smith, and the Crown Prince of Basketball himself, Meadowlark Lemon. Never in my life would I have imagined being in the same gym with these basketball greats. I quickly learned that Meadowlark, who ran the training camp, was not the same carefree funny guy that I watched from the stands at the Omaha Civic auditorium in my youth, or on the Saturday morning cartoon, Scooby Doo, for that matter.

There was no laughing or playing around. It was all business. Meadowlark was in the process of putting together the greatest comedic basketball teams in the world. While in training camp he had a method of creating perfection and making sure the show was executed with precision. Management was only looking at keeping two players, and those two needed to be able to make the fans go wild by dunking the basketball. Did I mention how I made the team? It would help if you knew as it will help give a better picture of my plight.

While working at Jack Ramsey's basketball camp, I met a

basketball player, Steve Flint. He stood out because he was a super tanned guy wearing a couple of nice gold chains around his neck. Gold chains were popular in the 80s. If you were a guy who wanted to look fly, you made sure to sport at least two. When I asked him where he got them, I was blown away when he said he bought them in Saudi Arabia when he played with Meadowlark Lemon's team The Shooting Stars. I couldn't believe what I was hearing! He proceeded to let me in on what I needed to do to try out for the team. I was excited about the opportunity, especially since my Boston Celtics tryout fell through as well as my chance to be a part of a USA basketball team tour of the Orient.

After presenting my stats to the team, I learned that they were very impressed. Back then we didn't have computers so everything was typed. All the numbers looked great except for one. There was a typo that listed me as being 6'9 instead of 5'9. Before the error was discovered, management agreed to pay all of my expenses, but that soon changed once they found out the real deal. After that, I was not on management's radar, but since I agreed to come anyway and take care of my expenses, they gave me a courtesy tryout. After 1 week and 2 days of grueling practices, Meadowlark signed me without consulting with management. Although this didn't sit well with them, and Meadowlark wasn't smiling yet, I was still appreciative because I knew he was giving me the opportunity to show what I had to offer. My excitement waned a bit when I leaned that there was a catch. The position I was given was not on the same team as Meadowlark, but with the team that was run over and made fun of by Meadowlark and the others. I tried not to let it bother me by focusing on the opportunity itself.

The season was very long. We had played approximately 150 games in 4 different countries. While it was exciting, it was also work. As a rookie, I remember having this constant feeling of doubt and insecurity about my being there. After all, I was still on probation and felt like I was walking a narrow line. I distinctly remember one particular game that helped me to understand my purpose on the team.

We were on a European tour and were to be in Sweden for 14 days. Whenever we played abroad we normally would schedule games with the hosting country's pro basketball team. We played this particular team right when we got off a 14-hour train ride from Copenhagen to the northern tip of Sweden. Needless to say, we were all out of it to some degree. From the very beginning, I didn't feel much like playing at all. When the game started, the home team didn't waste any time and jumped up to a twenty point lead. In order for us to put on a show, it was vitally important that we led the game, not the other way around. So there was no comedy going on. Instead, it appeared like the National team were toying with us.

Meadowlark was highly upset by this, and remained focused on trying to gain control of the game. The tension was mounting. Down the court they ran. On one particular play, the ball went up, bounced off the rim, and the center on the other team got the rebound. On his way down, he elbowed Meadowlark by mistake. Meadowlark had a few words with him. The ref urged them to move on, but the exchange was just the beginning. A few minutes later the guy elbowed Meadowlark again. This time, however, Meadowlark swung back, knocking the guy out. The other team's bench cleared and one of their players ran up and grabbed Meadowlark who handled him in-kind, and I was right in the middle of it! This little guy from Omaha, had never been that scared before. There I was, thousands of miles away from my home and family, in a brawl with a bunch of guys, I wasn't sure I would be sharing a court with next season.

The crowd grew wild and started throwing things at us, and we had to be rushed off the court. Back in the locker room, ranted about our performance and that of the opposing team. Then the promoter came in and told our team manager that Meadowlark could no longer play because of his conduct. Little did he know that team strategy always had Meadowlark sitting out in the 3rd quarter. After we had all calmed down, reassessed and caught our breaths, Meadowlark told us to kick butt until we smelled "dookie" and he would take care of the rest.

By the time we went back out to start the 3rd quarter, we were on fire and we ended up turning the game around. With 2 minutes remaining in the quarter, Meadowlark walks up to the counter and pushes the buzzard to come in. The crowd starts booing and the promoter starts yelling to the ref that Meadowlark was out of line and forbid him to play, not knowing that it was all a part of the show. The ref ignored the promoter and Meadowlark was allowed into the game despite all the jeers coming from the crowd. It's remarkable how the crowd response did not seem to affect him at all.

Within 2 minutes at the start of the 4th quarter, a lady got up to leave and Meadowlark called out to her, "Hey lady!" but she ignored him. He called out to her again, but she kept walking faster this time as if she knew she was being picked on. With a shrug of his shoulders, he simply yelled out, "Well, when you gotta go, you gotta go!" (Implying that she was leaving to use the restroom). Someone laughed in response and before we knew it, the whole crowd joined in. A kid saw Meadowlark interacting with the woman and wanted to join in the fun. He stood up to clown around too, but before he could, Meadowlark called out in a silly voice, "Sit down kid!" and the crowd went crazy; only this time in a very positive way. From that point on, the crowd intently watched Meadowlark's every move to catch a funny moment for an opportunity to laugh. They even tried to coax him into coming to their side of the gym for personal laughs.

The last 15 seconds of the game Meadowlark asked for the ball in the back court. I passed him the ball at the hash mark about 75 feet from the basket. The crowd starts counting down, "10, 9, 8, 7, 6..." when Meadowlark yells out, "A tiskit a tasket I think I'll make a basket!" He proceeded to let loose this 75 foot hook shot and before it hits the rim he takes off for the locker room while the ball hit nothing but net!

If I wasn't there I would not have believed it. We all ran to the locker room totally unlike we had entered before. Meadowlark taught me a valuable lesson that night. No matter the odds against you, no matter the leers or the jeers. No matter if friends, teammates or even family leaves you, the show must go on! From that day on, I decided that I would always put on the best show.

The Ball Is In Your Court

While each of these great coaches' contributions impacted me in different ways, there is a common theme that is thread throughout. They all deemed it necessary to turn each moment into a teachable one for me. This special attention demonstrated that there is always a better way to get something done, but we have to be willing to set aside tradition to get there. One doesn't have to stay in a box to get results. What could have happened to me if I rebuffed Coach Martin's correction? "The way of a fool seems right in his own eyes, but a wise man is he who listens to counsel." Just as the wise saying states, a man who can't take correction is a fool.

Leadership is doing what's right even when it looks wrong, and willing to look wrong when you are really right, while being quiet about it. The path to greatness is the road less travelled. Loneliness is your companion, and truth will be your guide. With leadership, you have to be willing to suffer alone.

Every good leader realizes that sometimes risks are required to get the deal done, to grow the business, or to bring the dream into fruition. It takes a person who is tired of being ordinary, or living a mediocre existence to take a bold stand. Each of my coaches brought value to my relationship with them. They were willing to step outside of the box. Yes, even Dan Johnson.

INVESTING

"It's true that charisma can make a person stand out for a moment, but character sets a person apart for a lifetime."
~John Maxwell

Faith is the substance of things hoped for, the evidence of things not seen. It is amazing how believing in people can push them to higher heights. In the world where people hide behind the church walls, choirs and pulpits, it's good to know that there are actually people who exemplify faith and long suffering. These individuals live beyond themselves. They put in great time and effort to make the difference in other's lives.

> "...don't judge me by anything other than my actions. And in five years' time let's look back and see whether our actions were authentic, whether we actually served young people, whether we created opportunity."
> *Gerald Chertavian, CEO of Year Up*

Where do you fall in the lives of the people around you? Are you builder? Or a destroyer? Do you finish the race? Or come up with excuses that support you quitting? Do you run and hide in the multitude of quitters, or are you man or woman enough to stand all by yourself in the face of adversity? Faith has to be one of the most quoted words and also the one of most misused words. Where is your faith?

Pistol Pete Maravich

"You can't move forward if you're always looking in the rear view mirror."

It was 1986 and we were in Fountain Valley, CA at the Los Caballeros resort the start of my first tour with the Meadowlark Lemon's Shooting Stars. As a rookie, I had to endure the duties that came with the title. I carried the team bags and had to sit in the back of the bus next to the restroom squashed between two 6'8 teammates. I remember looking to the front of the bus and the star players Meadowlark, Curly, Gator, Vince Humphries, Ernest Aughburn and other veterans who had whole rows to themselves. After about 3 weeks of this seating assignment, and almost 20 bus rides, I realized things were going to have to change.

One day while warming up before the game, Pistol asked me if I wanted to play a game of 'horse.' I had seen him play many times on TV when the NBA hosted a Saturday show with players playing horse against one another. I accepted the challenge with joy. Hey! How many people could say, they played horse against Pistol Pete? Pistol won the first couple of games but that would soon change. I started to realize that his legs were not as strong as they once were, so all my shots would have to be athletic ones. This soon became our ritual before every game and we formed a pretty good friendship that would eventually get me out of what I called the projects (the back of the bus) and into the suburbs (the front of the bus).

The one thing Pistol loved to talk about was his father and his upbringing. These conversations would go on for hours and no one ever questioned me being in the 'burbs.' Soon I had temporary housing. We would talk about his childhood growing up and the different things that his dad would do to help him become a better player.

I was into dried apricots, and he was into health food, so whenever the bus reached a stop, we would hit the Mall in search of health food stores while the other players would scour around looking for pretty girls to give their comp tickets to. When they saw Pistol coming their way, they would leave because they knew he was a preacher and that he would mess up any action they could potentially have.

Pistol was so on fire for God that he didn't participate in anything that could compromise his beliefs. He refused to go to beaches or any questionable environments that would bring on temptation. He once tried to convince me to get a design of a cross shaved into my hair. During the 80's it was popular for the brothers to get parts or head designs shaved into their hair. I thought that was cool and had one in my hair for about a week without anyone realizing that it was a cross. Regardless, if anyone noticed it or not, I knew and Pistol knew and that was all that mattered.

On many occasions, Pistol and I would have many long conversations about his three favorite topics: God, life, and basketball. I admired his commitment to his faith because he not only talked about it, but walked it out every day. One day while on the bus, he was reading the newspaper and learned that he had just been inducted into the Naismith Hall of Fame. I congratulated him, but he quickly stopped me. With a serious expression on his face, he told me that no award was more important than the reward he would get from God. He talked about how players got so caught up in pleasing people, and being sold out to a game that would give them nothing back in return. He said that he didn't want to play 10 years in the NBA and die of a heart attack by age 40 from the drugs and lifestyle he had lived. He said, "Pee Wee," in that southern accent. "You have to realize that a man is not defined by the multitudes of what he does on the court, but by what he does off the court, and brother I'm off the court." I never really understood what he was saying until years later.

Our next game was at LSU known as the house that Pistol built. Dale Brown was the coach and he had two promising young basketball stars on his team Chris Jackson and Shaquille O'Neal. This was the first time I believe that Pistol had been back to the school since they fired his dad as coach. I remember him telling me that he was a little bitter when it came to the school. Well Pistol set aside his differences and went out to put on a memorable show that night. Afterwards, he did the unthinkable; he actually got the crowd together to pray. He really showed me that it really wasn't about basketball as much as it was about the people. He walked away from the court on his terms.

The last time I played with him was in Minneapolis, Minnesota. We were on our way back to Louisiana where I met his wife and two sons, Jaeson and Joshua. We sat next to each other on the plane, and had a great conversation about life. Pistol was 40 years old when and on January 5, 1988 while playing in a church pickup game he went up for a shot, had a heart attack and died. He left this earth just the way he said he would, but on the court which made him famous while making a bigger statement with the men he was playing with off the court.

Bill Laird

"White men can do more than jump!"

Basketball was one of the biggest draws at Creighton Prep. There were only 8 brothers (African Americans) who attended Prep at the time and we stuck together. One way we did that was through basketball. We played before school, during lunch, and after school. We mimicked the fancy moves and difficult shots of the NBA players that we idolized at the time. Every now and then some of the white guys wanted to join in the fun and we'd let them. Well, one day we got the most unusual request.

He was an odd looking fellow with wild curly hair carelessly tucked into a headband like John McEnroe. He sported knee length socks, making him look out of place like a nerd. We just knew this was going to be a joke. But this guy wasn't a fellow student. No, he was one of the teachers, Bill Laird.

When he came over to guard me, I just knew I was going to wax him. Man was I wrong! From jump street he was on me like stank on a gorilla. I never got such a butt whooping from any player let alone some old white guy. He must have felt juiced from his performance because he showed up the next day, and the next. Pretty soon he was like a regular fixture and each time he was on me, pushing me to my limit and beyond.

After a while of playing, we started to develop a relationship outside of basketball. This would be my first trusting relationship with a white man. There were still a lot of misconceptions about going to a predominantly white school. We had a saying that in atmospheres like Prep, you had to be twice as good as the white students just to get respect. One area I knew that they did not have a leg up on me was sports.

I wanted to show off my athletic abilities, and when my cousin Kerry Trotter suggested that we go out for the freshman football team past the initial tryout date, I jumped at the chance. Apparently, football wasn't going to be Kerry's thing and he quit after the first practice. I was tempted to leave myself when I looked up into the stands and noticed Bill Laird sitting there observing. Just like when we played basketball, he would continue to show up for my practices every day. He seemed to notice something in me that I hadn't yet tapped into. Because basketball was my first love, I was very limited in my football knowledge and experience. Mr. Laird was very proactive in supporting me by showing up not only during school, but after as well.

My freshman season turned out to be pretty good. I led the league in most yards average going from sideline to sideline. (Meaning I ran from sideline to sideline instead of end zone to end zone) I didn't gain too many all-purpose yards, but I was very entertaining to watch.

By the time the championship games arrived, I was excited about getting the chance to show off my skills. The other team won the coin toss and elected to receive. I was on the kickoff team. The punt was off! I was running full speed through a crowd of players, looking for the guy carrying the football, when all of a sudden this big guy side swiped me, and I heard and felt a crack. I fell to the ground groaning and grasping my shoulder. As it turned out, I broke my shoulder, collar bone, and arm. I was devastated. I was out of the championship game, and because of the extent of my injuries, I knew that basketball was out too. I was heartbroken because the main reason I went to Prep was to play basketball. Instead, I would be reduced to being a spectator.

I was a real mess. I was depressed because I could no longer participate in the games during lunch and after school. I was limited to just watching, and as a result, my grades began to suffer worse than they already had.

Then one day, while watching pickup games, Mr. Laird told me to get my butt out there and play. At first I was apprehensive. I did not want to re-injure my arm, but something made me get out there anyway. Mr. Laird picked me on his team because no one else would pick me for obvious reasons. Immediately feelings of inferiority came over me. I started to think about all the times when playing ball in the neighborhood, I was overlooked because of my size. Now, I was a one-arm klutz. I couldn't handle the ball with my good left hand because it was my right shoulder that got broken, and I was right handed.

I was also nervous about looking bad on the court because I had never shot with my left hand. I was in uncharted territory, but Mr. Laird had a plan. He forced me to work with my left hand. He never said much, but kept passing me the ball forcing me to make plays. Over the remainder of the year we played together every day on the same team, and my confidence grew as did my skills. I noticed people around me starting to respect my game and there was talk and anticipation of what I would be like once I got my right hand back.

Mr. Laird took the time out to push me in my time of adversity. A time period when I could have given up and saw no value or purpose in my life. He showed me how to be innovative and creative. That year of not playing high school basketball was actually the foundation and formation of me becoming a successful basketball player and productive man in society. Mr. Laird not only jumped in to help me, but he has also been a very main stream force of encouragement and support in my family even until this day totally dispelling the fact that *white men can't jump.*

Tom Allen

"Remember to take study breaks."

Tom Allen was the father of Harry and Dan Allen. Dan played on the A Team for the Creighton Prep's freshman football team and was pretty good. He was what you would call a bull dog. He played defense and at that time he had braces on his teeth and his mouth would be full of blood while he would be bringing down the hammer on you. Off the field, he was the nicest guy you'd know. But when he played, man you wanted to stay away from him at all cost, even if you were on his team. Now Harry, his twin brother, was totally opposite. He was not particularly athletic, but he was pretty sharp when it came to school. He was the team trainer and took his job very seriously. He reminded me of Adam Sandler's character in the movie *The Water Boy*. Despite our differences, the three of us grew to be really good friends.

While playing in the championship game for the A team I broke my shoulder in the first quarter, and had to be taken to the hospital. While leaving the field I remember hearing a loud, raspy voice shout out, "Good job Harrison!" I didn't think anything of it because I didn't know who it was and I was in so much pain from my injury.

Later while at the hospital, waiting to be seen, I was surprised to hear that same raspy voice. "Hey, where can I find Les Harrison?" Before I knew it, the guy from the game was in my room and introducing himself to me and my mother. He was Tom Allen, the father of my friend's Harry and Dan. I was shocked that this big guy with the raspy voice had left the championship game in which his son was playing to make sure I wasn't in the hospital by myself. I think he even brought me some ice cream!

From that day on Mr. Allen would check on me every week to make sure that I stayed encouraged. When I transferred from Creighton Prep to Central High School, his support followed me there too. He would show up to my games and hang around at the end, say a few words, and shake my hand. I didn't understand his interest in attending Central games. Creighton Prep was the big ticket in town and we were, I felt, the bottom of the basement.

After high school Mr. Allen sent me a letter to check on me. It simply read, *never give up, take a study break, and get you something to eat.* Inside his letter of encouragement was a check for $25 which was big money in those days. This went on all throughout college. He would even find time to show up at my games and take me out to lunch or dinner afterwards. His letters and visits would be appreciated as well as those $25 checks. After graduating from college in my early adult years the $25 checks still came and were just as important and impactful to me as the very first time.

Mr. Allen was a wealthy man and could have given me much more than $25, but this was about more than charity, he was sowing a seed. He had given me $25 (every month) for over 15 years! Despite the fact that I had to leave Creighton Prep for academic reasons, and that I struggled to graduate from Central, followed by the fact that I had bounced around a couple colleges, Mr. Allen didn't give up on me. He always managed to locate me so that he could send the note and $25.

After college I started a company called *Voices Crying in The Wilderness.* Guess who gave me my first donation? That's right Mr. Allen. Only this time his wife stepped in and said, "You better give him more than $25!" For several years, I put on a camp for underprivileged kids, giving them a back pack filled with school supplies and an envelope containing a note of encouragement and $25. The first $25 that I received from Mr. Allen made me want to work hard and not quit. I felt like I had value during a time when the only people who believed in me were my parents. I needed someone else to believe in me when I didn't believe in myself. To this very day I strive to never give up, eat a good meal, and always take my study breaks.

Never believe that a few caring people can't change the world.
For, indeed, that's all who ever have.
~Margaret Mead

The Ball Is In Your Court

"When you give someone your time, you are giving them a portion of your life that you'll never get back. Your time is your life. That is why the greatest gift you can give someone is your time." This is a quote from Rick Warren's book, *The Purpose Driven Life*. I really like this quote because so often when one thinks about sowing or giving, they equate it to money. Giving of one's time is just as valuable, if not more. Like Rick Warren says, time is something that you have to give freely without a return. It is something that you cannot get back. You can always recoup money, but you can't recapture time.

Each of the men I mentioned in this chapter were natural givers. Pistol Pete gave me the heart to want to always do the right thing. Bill Laird gave me the desire to spend time and make a difference in the lives of young people. While money was the tool, Tom Allen taught me how to give, and to invest in those who don't necessarily look like you. Ask yourself, what kind of return are you getting on your investments?

EACH ONE, REACH ONE

*"Start where you are. Distant fields always look greener,
but opportunity lies right where you are. Take advantage
of every opportunity of service."*
~Robert J. Collier, Writer

 I n reflecting on my life, and those people who have made significant contributions, I am reminded of the song sung by the late great Whitney Houston titled *"The Greatest Love of All."* The words are below:

*I believe the children are our future.
Teach them well and let them lead the way.
Show them all the beauty they possess inside.
Give them a sense of pride to make it easier.
Let the children's laughter remind us how we used to be.*

I really don't know if people saw something special in me. I don't know if their actions were intentional, or by accident. I don't even know if each one remembers their exact contribution. I understand that I may never know these answers. What I do know is that each of these individuals greatly impacted my life in such a way that kept me dreaming and exploring new worlds and civilizations; to boldly go where no kid from Omaha had gone before. Being the second oldest of 11 kids, Lord knows I could use the help. My parents couldn't do it all, and I am sure that they appreciated the extra attention.

I hope that my experiences will motivate you to assist others, or look back over your life and recognize or acknowledge those stepping stones that laid the path for your own greatness. In addition, I encourage you to take a look around and see where you can personally touch, personally lend, or personally assist your fellow man.

I would like to thank all who have been a part of my life in various ways. You know who you are.

I want to say a special thanks to my sister, Lisa Harrison Jackson who is an author as well. Her encouragement and tireless support helped me to open my mind and tap into the writer within. I truly admire her creativity and patience. Talk about the perfect assist!

The game (life) is in session, the score (experience) is tied. The players (individuals) are growing exhausted, but know they can't quit. The team is hoping for a favorable outcome. The competition is tough. Despite this, they don't want to give up. With sweat pouring down their faces, they gulp down a cup of water and wipe their brows, ready to get back in. The buzzer goes off and they head on the court. Everyone is in place, but one. The only one missing in this quarter is YOU! It is your time. Now, suit up, put on your sneakers and let's get out there to pass that ball!

✠

GOOD *things come to those who believe,*
BETTER *things come to those who are patient,*
*and the **BEST** things come to those who don't give up!*
Never give up!

Why put in all the work and let someone else receive the benefits?
Truly the best is yet to come!

What will be your legacy? Will you be counted as one that fought until the end, or gave up when times got tough? You choose.

Never
Never
Never
Never
Give up!!

~Pee Wee Harrison

In Praise of Pee Wee Harrison's
Perfect Assist

This young man Les Harrison coming out of a small college in Oregon. He is from Omaha, NE. He sent us a memo wanting to play with Meadowlark and The Harlem Globetrotters along with Curly Neal. The memo said he was 6'9 instead of 5'9. I saw something great in him. He was a great defense player. The staff had some issues with him and gave him meaningless jobs. I took him under my wing. He played on the opposition team and he was so good that I had to put him on my team. The young kids love him. I named him Pee Wee and he didn't like it, but he soon became a household name. I truly value our friendship and proud to have mentored him and trained him in comedy basketball, because he was a very good player. Thanks Pee Wee for our 3 decade relationship

Meadowlark Lemon
Hall of Fame Harlem Globetrotter

As a nationally known basketball celebrity, Les "Pee Wee" Harrison is known all across America. Les specializes in delivering both powerful and uplifting messages that leaves people charged for life. My experience with Les's effect on children is phenomenal. He's a born leader with a natural value set that leads by example. I can't wait to read about some of his stories and life experiences being on the road with the world famous Meadowlark Lemon; the funniest man in basketball history.

Johnny "The Jet" Rodgers
Husker Player of the Century Heisman 1972
Hall of Fame '2000

First of all, please allow me to disclaim any attribution to me of a semblance of basketball prowess in this book, and then to give credit to his wonderful parents and brothers and sisters for their passes to him of the character he certainly has developed in his adult years. I delight in and am gratified by the credit he assigns to me for my small part in enabling him to become a person who has dished out so many perfect assists to others in his life.

Bill Laird,
Former Teacher
Creighton Preparatory High School

Our relationship unofficially began the night of my recruiting trip. George Fox University was playing Western Baptist College for a trip to nationals. The point guard that night was Les "Pee Wee" Harrison who would lead his team to defeat the team that would become my alma mater. A couple of years later I would meet in that infamous point guard and began to develop a friendship that would become a lethal duo on the court. As a player, I prided myself on the ability to finish and Les on getting us the ball in the right place, the perfect assist. When we started playing together I had to learn that Les was going to pass the ball to where "we needed to be" versus where "we thought we should be." His desire to get me in position to score with great passes was also something that he has done for me off the court. He has continued to challenge me to be myself, encouraged me to try things differently while always providing me with the support to have success. On the court I was a great finisher because of his assists and now off the court I am better man because of his assists. I'm not sure where he developed his "court vision" but I am so grateful to be on Pee Wee's team and to be the recipient of his perfect assists.

Cornelius Williams,
Friend, Brother-in-law & Former Teammate

What man can achieve except he try with all his might? Les is a friend whom you can rely on for many things except for despair and defeat. Les has suffered many losses but only because he has made many attempts. I am glad to know such a friend.

Rogers English,
Friend and Confidant

Watching Les and his beautiful assists on the court back in the mid-80's was a great experience for me as a college student and friend. When I fast forward to today. I see the same assistance in Les as he passes on wisdom to middle school students through his character education program as well as university students in the areas of life, sports career and intentional living. The Perfect Assist is a poignant call to live on purpose!"

Jeff Vanden Hoek,
Director of Business Relations, George Fox University

When Les transferred to Central High School, we became like brothers. Les would come over to my house and we'd play music by the Temptations. We loved The Temptations. Les was always Paul or Melvin Williams and I was David Ruffin. My Mother was single living in the projects, raising 9 kids. It was hard for her to get things we needed like clothes and food, but she did the best she could. Although he came from a large family too, Les would let me wear some of his golf shirts, which showed me then, that he was a true friend and always treated me as an equal. What he showed me then has never changed. As Les and I got older, he never forgot where he came from. He has always remained the same. I am very proud of the accomplishments he has made, especially when he was inducted into Central High School Hall of Fame.

Kenneth L. Matthews,
Friend

I always admired Les for his ability to make others around him feel important in his presence. Most players on a show team want and need to be the star, but not Les. He was great in helping his teammates achieve success. Because of this, he was recognized by Meadowlark and was moved from the opposing squad to the Shooting Stars! When that happened, Les became even more popular with the fans. Especially the kids. He has that infectious smile and a gift of making people feel better.

As Les become more popular, management sent him out to do advance work as well. Advance work is when a player arrives ahead of the team and promotes the game. Often times by doing hospital visits, radio and TV interviews, meet & greets at stores or restaurants, and most importantly school assemblies. Les became a star at these events. Not only because of his basketball skills, but his message and motivational speaking talent. He is the perfect assist!

Mark Shannon
Announcer, referee, & tour director
Adjunct Professor of
Communication

Pee Wee has been a good friend and teammate. I am proud of his many accomplishments. He always 'made them smile.'

Curly Neal
Hall of Fame Harlem Globetrotter

Since I have known Pee Wee Harrison he has always had an ability to connect with the people he comes in contact with. Over the years he has been involved in a number of my charity golf tournaments at which he is always a crowd favorite. I consider him a good friend. I look forward to getting to know more about my friend and reading the chapters of his life story.

Fergie Jenkins
MLB Hall of Fame pitcher

I have always admired Pee Wee's desire to learn. He has always been a great friend to me on and off the court. I'm so impressed with what he's done with his life as a basketball player and as a person. Even though we never actually played with one another on the Harlem Globetrotters team, our time together as Shooting Stars as well as a Harlem All Stars will always be very special to me.

Larry Gator Rivers
Harlem Globetrotter

SPECIAL THANKS

I'd like to thank the following people who made an impact in my life as well. While our memories are cherished, and shared stories worth telling, time will not allow me to do that. So, I honor you with a special listing with the hopes that you know that you are all in my heart and on my mind.

Pastor Brown & Family

Pastor Gino Jennings

Eric Etrain Lautenbach

Curtis Kimbrough

Greg Bolt

Brad Barbarick

Craig Moody

Pete and Lacy Arnett

Greg and Linda Carradine

Juliette

Trotter Family

Leslie Kampstra

Iverson & Family

Michelle Shaw

Chris Wulf

Carlos Gilyard

Willie Briscoe

Clark Buerk

Melissa Still

W. E Ghunniman

Janet Labanze

Rob Chavez

Jessica Haynes

Papa Williams

Mary & Trevor Tompkin

Michael Davis Jr.

Muntasar Rushdan

Mickey Brown

Young Family

Kevin Carroll

Crossley Family

Parks Family

Prince Family

Triplett Family

Watson Family

Cotton Family

Theresa Davis & Family

Dania Smith & Family

Stovall Family

Self Enhancement Family

Brian Littlejohn

Desmond Taylor

Doc Titus

Scotty Harris

McDaniel Family

Pres. Ed Stevens & Family

E Baby Kiem

Ron Phillips

Nate Phillips

Pee Wee's Favorite Quotes to Ponder...

- *You don't know what you're missing until someone gives you something you never had.*
- *An opinion is nothing but an opinion until it meets up with a fact. Then it's either true or false.*
- *Small minds talk about others big minds talk about ideas.*
- *Some people will always look at things to put you down instead of building you up.*
- *The enemy of good is great.*
- *Always meet people where they are.*
- *Timing is everything in leadership. The best leaders are when their maturity aligns with their ambition; when knowledge and temperament are in perfect harmony.*
- *One monkey don't stop the show. (Shirley Harrison)*
- *Fight battles that are big enough to make a difference but small enough to win!*
- *Better to obey God without an understanding then to disobey him with understanding.*
- *Don't base your decisions off the advice of people who don't have to deal with the results.*
- *It's better to be thought a fool then to speak and remove all doubt.*
- *Don't let your weapons grow faster than your knowledge.*
- *The path to greatness is the road less traveled, loneliness will be your companion and truth will be your guide.*
- *A man 'gots' to do what a man 'gots' to do. No a man 'gots' to do the right thing.*
- *Envy is a waste of time. Accept what you already have, not what you need.*
- *Count the cost and make sure you're not losing something costly.*
- *Always know if the juice is worth the squeeze.*
- *The more you think you see the easier it is to fool you.*
- *You can't make it up a hill if halfway up you turn around.*
- *Tell the truth and it becomes part of your past, tell a lie and it becomes part of your future.*
- *Make peace with your past so it won't screw up the present.*
- *You can never please God if you don't have the courage to evaluate yourself.*
- *Black holes are bottomless. Take hold before it's too late.*
- *Your million dollars is right in front of you.*
- *People will run from the truth and question everything, and run to a lie and question nothing.*

ABOUT THE AUTHOR

Les "Pee Wee" Harrison will challenge the audience to "Dream an Unrealistic Dream" and ask themselves, "Why Not"? Pee Wee's journey started in Omaha, Nebraska as the second child out of eleven. His strong family roots, core values, continual self-inquiry and inquisitive nature helped him avoid the pit falls of the streets and to navigate through a flawed educational environment, going on to college to earn his MBA. Pee Wee finally reached his dream of playing basketball alongside his childhood idols, Meadowlark Lemon and Curly Neal after both left the Harlem Globetrotters. Pee Wee has the longest tenure of playing aside Lemon, following Curly Neal, with a tenure of 28 years.

Pee Wee now has a nationally recognized Youth Character Education program (Anti-Bullying-A.P.P.L.A.U.S.E.) and inspires transitional change from Management to Leadership with his corporate motivational speaking. His audiences leave empowered to live out their dreams and encouraged to establish new concrete directions.

Les "Pee-Wee" Harrison is contagious. The energy, humor, insight and inspiration he brings to audiences, both small and large, cannot be denied. His unique multi-disciplined approach allows for connection with a wide range of audiences including students, educators, parents, and professionals. He is able to leave a lasting impression for affecting positive change. His messages will inspire to fulfill dreams, as well as to motivate and empower to action.

Pee Wee is a great fit for schools, organizations, and companies that are looking to provide an opportunity for their student body, employees and managers to be motivated towards the next level with courage, conviction and passion. Schools, churches, seminars, sales meetings and leadership training, his messages are customized to your needs.
For bookings, visit to www.peeweeharrison.net.

16414299R00039

Made in the USA
San Bernardino, CA
03 November 2014